TINY HOME BUILDERS' LEGAL HANDBOOK

LEGAL GUIDELINES FOR THE TINY-HOMES-ON-WHEELS INDUSTRY

Jenifer Levini, Esq.

**Copyright © 2022, Jenifer Levini, Esq.
All rights reserved.**

Limit of Liability/ Disclaimer of Warranty: This publication is designed to provide accurate and authoritative information in regard to the subject matter covered. The information you obtain in this book is not, nor is it intended to be legal advice. You should consult an attorney for individual advice regarding your own situation. The information in this book is not a substitute for personal or business legal advice. Please note that neither reading this book nor contacting the author creates an attorney-client relationship. While the author has used her best efforts in preparing this book, she makes no representations or warranties with respect to the accuracy or completeness of the contents of this book and specifically disclaims any implied warranties of merchantability or fitness for a particular purpose. The advice and strategies contained herein may not be suitable for your situation.

Levini Law Publishing

L

www.levini.com

TABLE OF CONTENTS

INTRODUCTION 1

CHAPTER 1 3

BUSINESS ENTITY FORMATION...3

CHAPTER 2 10

LICENSES TO BUILD OR SELL TINY HOMES..10

    Alabama 12

    Alaska..12

    Arizona 13

    Arkansas 13

    California 14

    Colorado 18

    Connecticut..19

    Delaware 20

    Florida...20

    Georgia...21

    Hawaii 21

    Idaho 22

    Illinois..22

    Indiana 23

    Iowa 23

    Kansas...23

    Kentucky 24

    Louisiana..24

    Maine 25

    Maryland 26

    Massachusetts 26

Michigan	27
Minnesota	27
Mississippi	28
Missouri	28
Montana	29
Nebraska	29
Nevada	30
New Hampshire	30
New Jersey	31
New Mexico	31
New York	31
North Carolina	32
North Dakota	33
Ohio	33
Oklahoma	33
Oregon	34
Pennsylvania	34
Rhode Island	35
South Carolina	35
South Dakota	36
Tennessee	36
Texas	37
Utah	38
Vermont	39
Virginia	39
Washington	40
West Virginia	40
Wisconsin	41

Wyoming 41
CHAPTER 3 43
CONTRACTS TO SELL TINY HOMES 43
    Parts of a contract 44
CHAPTER 4 51
LEMON LAWS 51
CHAPTER 5 54
THOW BUILDING STANDARDS 54
    ANSI Standard A119.5 58
    NFPA 1192 61
    Building Bigger? 63
    Building Codes 64
CHAPTER 6 65
LEGAL DISPUTES 65
    Small Claims 65
    Arbitration 65
    Lawsuits 66
CHAPTER 7 67
FAQs 67
CHAPTER 8 71
CONCLUSION 71

A small house is not merely as good as its larger correlate; it is better.

--Jay Shafer

INTRODUCTION

When Jay Shafer moved out of a 14-foot Airstream and decided to build his first tiny house, he was smacked by his first brush with the law. He came face to face with building codes called "minimum-size standards." He decided to side-step this code by putting his little home on wheels. Thus, he became not only the father of the tiny home movement, but the trail blazer of tiny home builders looking for ways around the law.

Maybe, because of this origin, manufacturing tiny homes is a business that attracts entrepreneurs with outlaw spirits. These entrepreneurs are shocked about the overhead and expenses they have to pay to manage a business. Building tiny homes isn't just the cost of labor and building supplies. There are dozens of other, ongoing overhead expenses required to make your business legal and to protect yourself from normal business liabilities. And, now that this industry has grown to a size where it touches millions of people, the law makers are taking notice which means law enforcement is about to become brutal.

The entire tiny home movement is, in many ways, a retort to having too many laws that create too many restrictions on housing and barriers to personal freedom. Yet, the industry is searching for laws to follow so that manufacturers can build and sell tiny homes.

They need customers to have confidence that they are buying homes that won't fall apart as they are transported down the road or have "black water" come up from the toilet or shower. Importantly, customer confusion has made it tough to sell tiny homes when some cost $25K and others cost $150K, and they seem comparable. When some builders are using new parts, carefully following building standards and having their tiny homes certified, while others nail together used parts and pretend that their work is on par with the careful builders, the playing field is not level. People are confused and potential customers won't spend money. Thus, all businesses suffer when the industry is not regulated.

The only way to level the playing field for all builders, is to have and enforce building standards, licensing and business laws.

This book explains the current legal landscape to help the Tiny Homes on Wheels (THOWs) industry come into legal compliance with current local, state and federal laws.

This book is not intended to help with all your business processes. Your business needs management, sales, marketing, advertising, finance, employees, taxes, billing, record keeping, bookkeeping, accounting, insurance and other operations which also have legal aspects, which are not covered in this first-edition handbook.

CHAPTER 1

BUSINESS ENTITY FORMATION

One of your first decisions after deciding to start a Tiny Home on Wheels (THOW) business is the "form" of your business. This is legal jargon for whether or not you will form an entity, or if the business will exist as part of you, without a separate entity. There are five different ways to form a business and they have major consequences on whether your business will be legal under your state's laws, whether you will be protected from liability, how you pay taxes and how much taxes you pay.

Basic business forms are C-Corporation (corp), S-Corporation, Limited Liability Company (LLC), sole proprietor, and partnership. The first three are formed by and recognized by your state as a separate entity. The last two are formed when you just start doing business without forming any legal entity, either by yourself or with a partner(s).

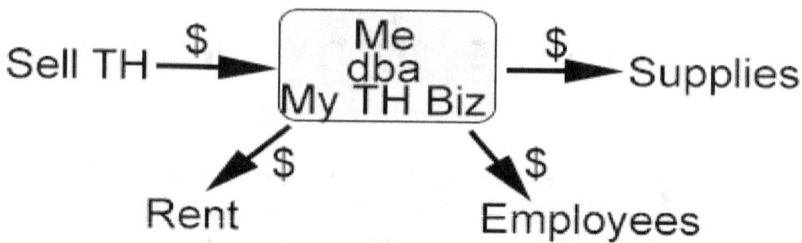

Sole Proprietorship or Partnership

THIS DIAGRAM SHOWS THE RESULTS OF DOING BUSINESS AS A SOLE PROPRIETOR (OR PARTNERSHIP). WHEN YOU SELL THOWS MONEY COMES INTO YOU OR YOUR BANK ACCOUNT. WHEN YOU PAY RENT, EMPLOYEES OR BUY SUPPLIES THAT COMES DIRECTLY FROM YOUR BANK ACCOUNT. UNDER THE LAW AND FOR TAXES, YOU AND THE BUSINESS ARE THE SAME ENTITY. YOU MAY CREATE A DBA (DOING BUSINESS AS) BY REGISTERING THE BUSINESS WITH YOUR LOCAL GOVT. BUT THAT DBA DOES NOT CREATE A SEPARATE ENTITY.

As I explain in more detail in the next chapter, if you are building THOWs, under the law you are a vehicle manufacturer. If you sell THOWs, you are a vehicle dealer. Each state has rules about which type of entity is required for vehicle manufacturers and/or vehicle dealers in order to obtain a license. You cannot necessarily choose which business form you want for your business. Vehicle manufacturers and vehicle dealers are required to be licensed. And in some states, the license requirements dictate which business form is required for a license. Insurance and bonding requirements may change depending on the type of entity you form.

Many states require vehicle manufacturers and/or vehicle dealers to form a c-corporation. This means you cannot legally build or sell THOWs if you are doing business as a sole proprietorship, a partnership or as an LLC. There is a list of the requirements for all 50 states in the next chapter. Most states require formation of a c-corporation for manufacturing any vehicles. Forming a c-corporation is an important step to protect you from liability in case something goes wrong in your business, like an employee cuts off a finger, or a buyer falls off a ladder and sues you.

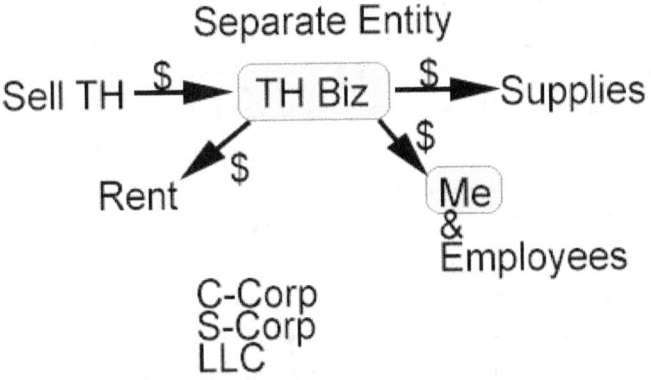

THIS DIAGRAM SHOWS THAT IF YOU FORM A C-CORPORATION, S-CORPORATION OR LIMITED LIABILITY COMPANY, IT IS AN ENTITY THAT EXISTS SEPARATE FROM YOU ("ME"). THE ENTITY ACCEPTS MONEY FROM SALES AND PAYS THE RENT, YOUR SALARY AND BONUSES, EMPLOYEES AND BUYS SUPPLIES.

What is a corporation? A corp is an entity. An entity has the same rights and responsibilities as a person. An entity has the right to enter and sign a contract, open bank accounts, borrow money, buy real estate, rent a building, and other business-related actions. An entity has the responsibility to pay its bill, follow the laws, not hurt any person or other entity, and follow the guidelines written into its corporate documents. The people who start and manage a corporation are called the officers: CEO, CFO, and COO, are the standard titles for the people in charge. A corp also has directors who hire and fire the officers. If it is a small, privately held corp, the officers and directors are the same person or people.

What is liability protection? A corp protects the officers and directors from liability. This means that if the corp gets sued, the CEO's personal wealth is not available as a remedy for the problem. For example, if you own a house and someone sues your corporation, your house cannot be taken away. Only the assets that belong to the corporation can be used to remedy damages. If the corp owns tools, someone who sues the corp could force the sale of the tools and be compensated that way.

Most people hire a lawyer to form their corporation. This is because a corporation requires writing complicated rules and documents that describe how the corporation will be managed, how the money and stock will be managed, and how the corporation will comply with state requirements. The articles of incorporation will be filed with your Secretary of State. And the Bylaws will be part of the corporate records. Whenever important actions or corporate changes are made, there must be a vote of the directors, officers or shareholders which is recorded on corporate minutes, written and signed on a corporate resolution. There are a lot of formalities in how it is managed which requires excellent record keeping. But, the good news about all that record keeping is that those records will likely keep you out of trouble as proof that you are following the rules, if anything goes wrong.

It is very important that once you form your corporation that you do all business in the name of the corporation, not your personal name, or you could lose the liability protection. For example, on your THOW sales contract, the agreement is between the corporation and the buyer. You will sign the contract as your name, the President or CEO, of the corp. When you open a bank account, you bring your Articles and Bylaws to the bank to show them that the corporation gave you the authority to open and manage the accounts. You must always include your title when you sign anything related to the business, to make sure everyone who you are contracting with understands that you are a representative of the corporation, not representing yourself. The utilities at your factory and the rental lease should be in the name of the corp. And payment of these bills should be from the corp's bank account. You get paid when the corp pays you a salary plus benefits.

If you accidently pay a bill with your personal account or put a bill in your name, that is called intermingling. Intermingling could cause you to lose the liability protection in a battle called piercing the corporate veil. So, it is important that you never intermingle personal and business money. If it happens, be sure to reimburse the account to undo the intermingling.

Another benefit of corporations is that they issue stock. Stock is the way that ownership is held. When you start your corp be sure to issue at least 10 million shares. Each share may have a value that is a small fraction of a cent at the time of issue. Having these shares will allow the corporation to get investment as a way to raise money. The shares can be sold to the investor. Another way to raise money is a convertible note. This means that you take out a loan from an investor, but if the company grows large and goes public that loan converts to stock which the lender can sell at a profit. In other words, you may not have to pay back the loan. These corporate techniques to raise money are only available after forming a c-corp. They are complicated and require guidance from a corporate lawyer.

	Sole Proprietor	Partner	C-Corp	S-Corp	LLC
Separate entity			X	X	X
Liability protection			X	X	X
Issue stock for investors			X	X	
Single taxes	X	X		X	X
Corp formalities			X	X	
Contracts	X-dba	X-dba	X	X	X
Bank accounts	X-dba	X-dba	X	X	X

SOME OF THE SIMILARITIES AND DIFFERENCES BETWEEN THE 5 BUSINESS FORMS.

The unfortunate thing about C-Corps is that they have to pay taxes just like a person. At tax time the corp will pay taxes and you will pay taxes. Basically, you're taxed twice on the company's income. You need to keep this in mind at the time you price your products because you could end up losing money every time you work if you don't understand how taxes work. You will need a good accountant to help you find the ways to minimize taxes.

Taxes

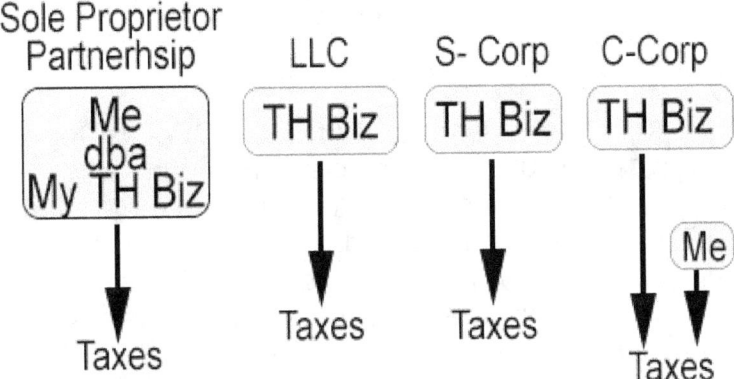

TAXES ARE ONE OF THE MOST IMPORTANT ASPECTS OF YOUR BUSINESS. YOU MAY THINK YOU MADE MONEY, THEN TAXES COME ALONG AND YOU BARELY BROKE EVEN. YOU WILL BECOME FRIENDS WITH YOUR ACCOUNTANT WHO WILL HELP YOU LEARN HOW TO MAKE BUSINESS DECISIONS WITH TAXES IN MIND. C-CORPORATION ARE SUBJECT TO DOUBLE TAXATION. BOTH THE COMPANY AND YOU PAY TAXES ON THE INCOME.

CHAPTER 2

LICENSES TO BUILD OR SELL TINY HOMES

A business that **builds** THOWs is legally called a vehicle manufacturer or "manufacturer." A business that **sells** THOWs is legally called a vehicle dealership or "dealer." The laws that govern licensing and bonding for manufacturers and dealers are different in every state. And the laws vary depending on the type of tiny home(s) you're building. There are three types of tiny homes on wheels, and they have different licensing laws in each state. The three types of THOWs are THOW-RV (RV size is either a travel trailer or fifth-wheel body style), THOW-PM (park models are larger than RVs), and THOW-MH (manufactured homes are the largest being wider and longer and multiple units can be joined together.)

If you intend to build and/or sell THOWs, you will have frequent contact with many of your state's agencies to get the required licenses and permits and to collect and pay taxes. You must follow various regulations. You may be required to be bonded (a type of insurance), to form a corporation, obtain a license, get permits, collect and pay taxes. The following pages detail some of, but not all the information you need to find those agencies and get started on these processes.

Obviously, the rules are different if you're manufacturing versus selling THOW-RV, THOW-PM or THOW-MH. 32 states require THOW-RV manufacturers to get a state license. But only seven states require THOW-RV manufacturers to be bonded. 28 states require THOW-PM manufacturers to get a state license. But only eight states require THOW-PM manufacturers to be bonded. 34 states require THOW-MH manufacturers to get a state license. But only seven states require THOW-MH manufacturers to be bonded.

For dealers, all 50 states require a state vehicle dealers license to sell THOW-MH, 44 states require this license to sell THOW-RV and 40 states require this license to sell THOW-PM. 46 states require THOW-PM dealers to be bonded, 40 for THOW-RV, and 35 for THOW-PM. Typically vehicle dealer & manufacturer licenses are managed via the Department of Motor Vehicles (DMV). The dealership licensing process can take several months, require testing and criminal background checks. Business licenses are managed by the motor vehicles bureau, treasury or Secretary of State, depending on your state. You may also need a local business license or registration wherever you open your dealership or manufacturing facility. Corporate formation is managed via the Secretary of State. The State Treasurer collects taxes. Some states have business start-up portals that link to many business resources. Consider hiring specialists to help with these processes such as lawyers, accountants, a payroll company, and business consultants.

Some states prohibit a single company from being both a manufacturer and a dealer, selling its own vehicles. These antitrust laws will need to be challenged by the tiny home industry where most manufacturers also sell their vehicles. But you're not alone. Tesla also manufactures and sells their own vehicles. If we're lucky, Tesla will challenge these laws, and pave the way for tiny home manufacturers to sell their vehicles legally.

Here are the state-by-state requirements for licensing and bonding, with links to the agencies where you can get the paperwork:

Alabama

> Alabama requires all manufacturers to be licensed but not bonded. Only THOW-MH dealers need to be licensed and have a $25,000 bond.
> Manufacturers Licensing: https://revenue.alabama.gov/business-license/faq/
> Dealers Licensing: Dealer License – Alabama Department of Revenue
> Motor Vehicle Department: Motor Vehicle – Alabama Department of Revenue
> Form a corporation: Corporate Income Tax FAQ – Alabama Department of Revenue
> Transportation: ALDOT - Home (state.al.us)

Alaska

> Alaska requires all manufacturers to be licensed but not bonded. All dealers must be licensed and have a $50,000 bond.
> Licensing: Business Licensing Forms & Fees, Business Licensing, Division of Corporations, Business and Professional Licensing (alaska.gov)
> Dealer requirements:

Dealer & Buyer's Agent Requirements, Division of Motor Vehicles, Department of Administration, State of Alaska

Business Development: Finance Section, Division of Economic Development (alaska.gov)

Forming a corporation: Division of Corporations, Business and Professional Licensing (alaska.gov)

DMV: http://doa.alaska.gov/dmv/

Arizona

Arizona requires all manufacturers to be licensed but not bonded. All THOW dealers need to be licensed and have a $100,000 bond.

Transportation: https://azdot.gov/

Motor Vehicles Dept: https://servicearizona.com/

Licensing: https://azdor.gov/transaction-privilege-tax/tpt-license/license-fees-cancellation-and-other-changes

Form a corporation: https://www.azcommerce.com/programs/small-business-services/

Arkansas

Arkansas requires all manufacturers to be licensed but not bonded. All THOW dealers need to be licensed and have a $50,000 bond.

Licensing: https://www.amvc.arkansas.gov/

Business support: https://www.dfa.arkansas.gov/cba/businesses

Dealer licensing:

https://www.dfa.arkansas.gov/images/uploads/motorVehicleOffice/DealerInformationSheet.pdf

State Contacts: https://www.dfa.arkansas.gov/contact-info

Form a corporation: https://www.ark.org/sos/ofs/docs/index.php

Transportation: http://www.arkansashighways.com/

California

Vehicle manufacturers must be licensed by the State of California Department of Motor Vehicles (DMV) but not bonded. In the licensing process, the state will conduct a background investigation to make sure you do not have any criminal convictions or acts of moral turpitude related to vehicle sales. If you've been convicted or pled nolo contendere, your application can be refused. To secure your license, you're required to

- file an application,
- pay the fees, and
- explain which dealers you will be selling your vehicles.

The application must include photos of your manufacturing facilities, a brochure about your manufactured product, proof that your articles of incorporation are in good standing with the secretary of state, and an inspection of your offices. The investigation process takes about four months. The application instructions can be found at the DMV website

https://www.dmv.ca.gov/portal/wcm/connect/a018dbc6-3e08-4a7f-8255-

b9f192e5fdcd/ol307.pdf?MOD=AJPERES

THOW dealers must be licensed and have a $50,000 bond. You'll go through the same highly regulated process as someone opening a car dealership. There is a lot of crime in the car sales industry from used car dealers to auto dismantlers and importers/exporters. Thus, do not be surprised when you are treated with suspicion.

You must decide at the license application phase whether you will be brokering or selling new or used vehicles. New vehicle dealers are allowed to sell both new and used vehicles.

If you're selling new THOW, you'll have to meet the standard requirements of the manufacturer. Proof of meeting the standard is usually provided by some sort of certificate of completion of a program. To sell used THOW, you'll have to take a course from the DMV, specifically for RV dealers.

During the licensing application process, the state will fingerprint you and conduct a background investigation to make sure you do not have any criminal convictions or acts of moral turpitude related to vehicle sales. Again, if you've been convicted or pled nolo contendere, your application can be refused. This investigation is done to help avoid licensing people who may turn out to be unethical dealers.

You must acquire a surety bond, insurance, and a certificate of proposed franchise, as well as provide a lot of financial information.

The state inspectors will visit your sales location, even if you plan to primarily sell online. Photographs of your location must accompany your application. Your sales lot must pass inspection, and all vehicles on your website must be displayed at this commercial space. Any buildings must be permanent. Signs are also inspected to make sure they are of a permanent nature, erected on the exterior of the office or on the display area, and constructed or painted and maintained so as to withstand reasonable climatic effects.

Not surprisingly, like all state processes, there are fees associated with every step of the process. Expect to spend at least $800 for your license and to wait about four months for approval. The license must be renewed every other year. This is strictly enforced.

The state published a handbook to help navigate the entire DMV dealership application process, http://www.dmv.ca.gov/portal/dmv/detail/pubs/reg_hdbk_pdf/toc/.
The steps and application are available online at https://www.dmv.ca.gov/portal/dmv/detail/vehindustry/ol/dealer.
In addition to the license requirements specific to selling tiny homes, you'll also need to follow general state regulations regarding establishing a business entity.

To get a sellers' permit, apply for a business license, find out about collecting taxes, and learn more about forming a corporation, visit the state of California business portal, http://www.ca.gov/DoingBusiness.

Information about forming a corporation is also available from the secretary of state's office, http://www.ca.gov/Agencies/Secretary-of-State/Agency-Services/Form-a-Business.

A local attorney can help you as well.

Information about state taxes is available here, https://www.taxes.ca.gov/Income_Tax/newind.shtml. You can also seek guidance from a knowledgeable CPA.

You might also need to interact with other departments for the following:

Consumer Protection—
http://www.dca.ca.gov/

Highway Patrol—
https://www.chp.ca.gov/home/

Revenue—
https://www.taxes.ca.gov/Income_Tax/newind.shtml

Transportation—
https://www.taxes.ca.gov/Income_Tax/newind.shtml

Vehicle Dealer Licensing—
https://www.dmv.ca.gov/portal/vehicle-industry-services/occupational-licensing/occupational-licenses/vehicle-dealer-license/

Vehicle Manufacturers License—
https://www.dmv.ca.gov/portal/dmv/?1dmy&urile=wcm:path:/dmv_content_en/dmv/vehindustry/ol/manufacturer

If you can't find what you're looking for on this list, the following link connects you to all state agencies—
http://www.ca.gov/Agencies/Secretary-of-State/Agency-Services/Form-a-Business
If you're feeling frustrated about this business process, go directly to the governor's office that helps businesses get their permits, Cal Gold, http://www.calgold.ca.gov/.

Colorado

Colorado requires manufacturers of THOW-MH and THOW-RVs to be licensed but not THOW-PM. Manufacturers are not required to be bonded. THOW-MH and THOW-RV dealers need to be licensed and have a $50,000 bond. THOW are considered motor vehicles, under Colorado's definition:

"Motor vehicle" means every vehicle intended primarily for use and operation on the public highways which is self-propelled and every vehicle intended primarily for operation on the public highways which is not driven or propelled by its own power but which is designed to be attached to or become a part of or to be drawn by a self-propelled vehicle, not including farm tractors and other machines and tools used in the production, harvesting, and care of farm products.

To obtain a vehicle dealers license in Colorado requires:

- Have a net worth of at least $100,000;
- Have a vantage score of at least 701 through Experian;
- Pass a fingerprinting criminal background check, or provide supporting court documents if you have been convicted of a felony or misdemeanor;
- Application;
- Pay license fee;
- Pre-license certification;
- Pass an exam;
- Obtain a surety bond;
- Submit a business plan;
- Submit a copy of your lease;
- Submit your franchise agreement from the manufacturer;
- Sales tax license;
- Completed dealer checklist;
- And other steps may apply see

https://www.colorado.gov/pacific/enforcement/dealer-and-wholesaler-motor-vehicle-powersports-auto-industry-division

To obtain a manufacturer's license:
https://www.colorado.gov/pacific/sites/default/files/DR%202900_e_1.pdf

Fees for auto industry licensing:
https://www.colorado.gov/pacific/enforcement/fee-schedule-auto-industry-division

Starting a business:
https://mybiz.colorado.gov/intro

Transportation: https://www.codot.gov/

Connecticut

Connecticut requires all manufacturers to be licensed but not bonded; And all THOW dealers to be licensed and have a $50,000 bond.

Licensing: https://portal.ct.gov/DMV/Dealers-and-Repairs/Dealers-and-Repairs/Licensed-Dealers-and-Repairers-in-Connecticut

Business startup: https://portal.ct.gov/DRS/Businesses/Business-Tax-Page/Starting-a--New-Business

Delaware

Delaware requires all manufacturers to be licensed but not bonded. All THOW dealers need to be licensed but not bonded.

Manufacturers Licensing: https://delcode.delaware.gov/title30/c027/index.shtml & https://delcode.delaware.gov/title6/c049/index.shtml

Dealers Licensing: https://www.dmv.de.gov/VehicleServices/dealers/index.shtml

Motor Vehicle Department: https://www.dmv.de.gov/VehicleServices/index.shtml

Form a corporation: https://corp.delaware.gov/

Florida

Florida requires all manufacturers to be licensed and carry a $10,000 bond. All THOW-dealers need to be licensed and have a $10,000 bond if they have fewer

than four locations, or a $20,000 bond if 4 locations or more.
Laws in Florida are summarized on the RV dealer's association website: https://kb.frvta.org/dealermanufacturer-law/ and http://kb.frvta.org/
DMV: http://www.hsmv.state.fl.us/
Business startup: https://dos.myflorida.com/sunbiz/start-business/
Forms are available: https://kb.frvta.org/forms-needed-in-a-deal-and-steps-to-follow/

Georgia

Georgia requires all manufacturers to be licensed but not bonded. All THOW dealers need to be licensed but not bonded.
Manufacturers Licensing: https://dor.georgia.gov/motor-vehicles/dealer-distributor-manufacturer-transporter-license-plates/motor-vehiclemotorcycle
Motor Vehicle Department: https://dds.georgia.gov/
Form a corporation: https://ecorp.sos.ga.gov/
Business startup guide: https://georgia.gov/starting-business-guide

Hawaii

Hawaii only requires THOW-MH manufacturers and dealers to be licensed, but not bonded. Bond requirements are $50,000 for fewer than 10 units, and $200,000 for more than 10 units.
Licensing: http://cca.hawaii.gov/pvl/

Motor Vehicle Department: county-by-county information
Tax information: https://portal.ehawaii.gov/business/tax-services/
Business startup: https://portal.ehawaii.gov/business/starting-a-business/

Idaho

Idaho requires all manufacturers to be licensed but not bonded. All dealers need to be licensed and have a $20,000 bond.
Manufacturers Licensing: https://itd.idaho.gov//wp-content/uploads/2016/06/3172.pdf
Dealers Licensing: https://itd.idaho.gov//wp-content/uploads/2016/06/3170.pdf
Motor Vehicle Department: https://itd.idaho.gov/itddmv/
Form a corporation: https://sos.idaho.gov/business-forms/
Business incentives: https://commerce.idaho.gov/incentives-and-financing/grants/

Illinois

Illinois does not require manufacturers to be licensed or bonded. Manufacturers must register with the Secretary of State and pay a fee. All THOW dealers need to be licensed and have a $20,000 bond.
Dealers Licensing: https://www.cyberdriveillinois.com/publications/pdf_publications/vsd324.pdf & https://www.cyberdriveillinois.com/publications/pdf_publications/vsd659.pdf
Motor Vehicle Department: https://www.cyberdriveillinois.com/

Form a corporation: https://apps.ilsos.gov/corparticles/
Business startup: https://www2.illinois.gov/dceo/smallbizassistance/beginhere/pages/default.aspx

Indiana

Indiana only requires THOW-PM manufacturers to be licensed and carry a $25,000 bond. All THOW dealers need to be licensed and have a $25,000 bond.

Dealers Licensing: https://www.in.gov/sos/dealer/3284.htm & Motor Vehicle Bureau: https://www.in.gov/bmv/
Form a corporation: http://www.in.gov/sos/business/2426.htm
Business startup: https://inbiz.in.gov/start-business/step-one/

Iowa

Iowa requires all manufacturers to be licensed but not bonded. All THOW dealers need to be licensed. THOW-RV dealers require a $25,000 bond and a $75,000 bond for THOW-MH.

Dealers Licensing: https://iowadot.gov/mvd/buyingselling/buyingselling/trailer
Motor Vehicle Department: https://iowadot.gov/mvd
Form a corporation: https://sos.iowa.gov/file/origination/index.aspx
Business startup: https://sos.iowa.gov/business/StartingABusiness/search.aspx
Revenue Dept: https://tax.iowa.gov/

Kansas

Kansas requires all manufacturers to be licensed but not bonded. All dealers need to be licensed and have a $30,000 bond.
Manufacturers Licensing: see dealers license forms
Dealers Licensing: https://www.ksrevenue.org/pdf/d17a.pdf , https://www.ksrevenue.org/pdf/dlrhb-complete.pdf & https://www.ksrevenue.org/pdf/d20.pdf
Motor Vehicle Department: https://www.ksrevenue.org/dovindex.html
Form a corporation: https://www.kansas.gov/businesscenter/
Business startup: https://www.kcsourcelink.com/guides/start-a-business/register-and-license-your-business/starting-a-business-in-kansas

Kentucky

Kentucky requires THOW-RV an -MH manufacturers to be licensed but not -PM manufacturers. No manufacturers are required to have bonds. Likewise, THOW-MH and -RV dealers are required to be licensed. Dealers need not have bonds, but they must be insured.
Manufacturers Licensing: https://transportation.ky.gov/Organizational-Resources/Forms/TC%2098-2.pdf
Dealers Licensing: https://mvc.ky.gov/Pages/default.aspx
Motor Vehicle Department: https://drive.ky.gov/Pages/default.aspx
Form a corporation: https://www.sos.ky.gov/bus/business-filings/Forms/Pages/default.aspx

Startup Business: https://onestop.ky.gov/start/Pages/default.aspx
Business incentives: https://ced.ky.gov/

Louisiana

Louisiana requires THOW-RV and -MH manufacturers to be licensed but not bonded. THOW-PM manufacturers may need to be licensed. All dealers need to be licensed and have a $20,000 bond.

Manufacturers & Dealers Licensing: http://www.lmvc.la.gov/

Form a corporation: https://www.revenue.louisiana.gov/Businesses/BusinessRegistration

Business startup: https://www.sos.la.gov/BusinessServices/StartABusiness/Pages/default.aspx

Maine

Maine does not require THOW-RV or -PM manufacturers to be licensed or bonded. THOW-MH must be licensed. All dealers must be licensed, and bonded based on sales projections: 0-50 sales—$5,000, 51-100 sales—$10,000, 101-150 sales—$15,000, 151-200 sales—$20,000, Over 201 sales—$25,000.

Dealers Licensing: https://www.maine.gov/sos/bmv/forms/index.html#dealer &

https://www.maine.gov/sos/bmv/dealer/index.html

THOW-MH manufacturer & dealer licensing: https://www.maine.gov/pfr/professionallicensing/professions/manufactured-housing-board

Motor Vehicle Bureau: https://www.maine.gov/sos/bmv/
Business startup: https://www.maine.gov/portal/business/starting.html & https://www.maine.gov/portal/business/licensing.html

Maryland

Maryland requires all manufacturers to be licensed (see licensing fees), and bonded (1-50 veh $25,000; 51-500 veh $50,000; 501-10,000 veh $100,000; 10,000+ veh $300,000). All dealers must be licensed and bonded (1-50 veh $25,000; 51-500 veh $50,000; 501-10,000 veh $100,000; 10,000+ veh $300,000).

Manufacturers Licensing:
Dealers Licensing: https://mva.maryland.gov/businesses/Documents/New-Vehicle-Dealer-Business-Licensing-Packet.pdf ;
THOW-RV & -PM
https://mva.maryland.gov/businesses/Documents/Trailer-Dealer-Business-License-Packet.pdf
Motor Vehicle Administration: https://mva.maryland.gov/vehicles/Pages/default.aspx
Form a corporation: https://egov.maryland.gov/businessexpress
Business startup: https://open.maryland.gov/business-resources/starting-a-business/

Massachusetts

Massachusetts does not require manufacturers to be licensed or bonded.

All dealers need to be licensed but not bonded.
Dealers Licensing: https://www.mass.gov/orgs/office-of-consumer-affairs-and-business-regulation
Motor Vehicle Department: https://www.mass.gov/orgs/massachusetts-registry-of-motor-vehicles
Business resources: https://www.mass.gov/starting-your-business
Business startup: https://www.mass.gov/starting-your-business

Michigan

Michigan does not require manufacturers to be licensed or bonded. All dealers must be licensed and bonded ($10,000 bond).
Manufacturers Licensing: https://www.michigan.gov/statelicensesearch/0,4671,7-180-24786_24819-81373--,00.html
Dealers Licensing: https://www.michigan.gov/sos/0,4670,7-127-1631_50304-116622--,00.html
Motor Vehicle Department: https://www.michigan.gov/sos/0,4670,7-127-96435---,00.html
Form a corporation: https://www.michigan.gov/lara/0,4601,7-154-89334_61343_36737---,00.html
Business startup: https://sbdcmichigan.org/start-a-business/

Minnesota

Minnesota does not require manufacturers to be licensed or bonded. All dealers must be licensed and bonded ($50,000 bond).

Dealers Licensing:
https://mn.gov/elicense/a-z/?id=1083-231321#/list/appId//filterType//filterValue//page/1/sort//order/
Motor Vehicle Department:
https://dps.mn.gov/divisions/dvs/Pages/default.aspx
Form a corporation:
https://mn.gov/deed/business/starting-business/organizing/forming-corporation.jsp
Business startup:
https://mn.gov/elicense/a-z/?id=1083-231321#/list/appId//filterType//filterValue//page/1/sort//order/

Mississippi

Mississippi only requires manufacturers of THOW-MH to be licensed but not bonded. Only THOW-MH dealers need to be licensed and have a $25,000 bond (single location) or $100,000 bond for multiple locations. In Mississippi the organization and each representative doing business with dealers must also be licensed as per MISS. CODE ANN. § 63-17-83.
Manufacturers & Dealers licensing & bonding: https://www.mmvc.ms.gov/
Motor Vehicle Department:
https://www.mmvc.ms.gov/
Form a corporation:
https://www.sos.ms.gov/businessservices/documents/business%20entities%20(clean).pdf
Business startup:
https://mississippi.org/services/entrepreneurs/

Missouri
> Missouri requires all manufacturers to be licensed but not bonded. Only THOW-MH dealers need to be licensed and have a $25,000 bond.
> Manufacturers Licensing: https://dor.mo.gov/forms/5308.pdf
> Dealers Licensing: https://dor.mo.gov/motorv/liendeal/ &
>
> https://dor.mo.gov/motorv/liendeal/documents/DealerOperatingManual.pdf
> Motor Vehicle Department: https://dor.mo.gov/motorv/
> Form a corporation: https://www.sos.mo.gov/business/corporations/forms.asp#gen
> Business startup: https://openforbiz.mo.gov/

Montana
> Montana requires all manufacturers to be licensed but not bonded. All THOW dealers need to be licensed and have a $50,000 bond.
> Manufacturers & Dealers Licensing: https://dojmt.gov/driving/dealers-forms/#433-manufacturer-license-forms
> Motor Vehicle Department: https://dojmt.gov/driving/
> Form a corporation: https://sosmt.gov/business/
> Business startup: https://marketmt.com/ & https://madeinmontanausa.com/

Nebraska
> Nebraska requires all manufacturers to be licensed but not bonded. All THOW

dealers need to be licensed and have a $25,000 bond.
Manufacturers Licensing:
https://mvdealerbd.nebraska.gov/rep.html
&
https://mvdealerbd.nebraska.gov/pdfs/Rep_Lic_app.pdf
Dealers Licensing: https://mvdealerbd.nebraska.gov/dealer.html
Motor Vehicle Department: https://dmv.nebraska.gov/
Form a corporation: https://sos.nebraska.gov/business-services/new-business-information
Business startup: https://www.nebraska.gov/osbr/index.cgi

Nevada

Nevada requires all manufacturers to be licensed and bonded ($100,000 bond). All THOW dealers need to be licensed and have a $100,000 bond.
Manufacturers & Dealers Licensing: https://dmvnv.com/olbl.htm#Vehicle & https://dmvnv.com/pdfforms/obl243.pdf
Motor Vehicle Department: https://dmvnv.com/index.htm
Form a corporation: https://www.nvsilverflume.gov/startBusiness
Business startup: https://www.nvsos.gov/sos/businesses/start-a-business

New Hampshire

New Hampshire does not require manufacturers to be licensed or bonded. Only THOW-MH dealers need to be licensed and have a $25,000 bond.

Dealers Licensing: https://www.nh.gov/safety/divisions/dmv/registration/dealers/retail.htm
Motor Vehicle Department: https://www.nh.gov/safety/divisions/dmv/
Form a corporation: https://sos.nh.gov/corporation-ucc-securities/corporation/
Business startup: https://www.nh.gov/business/

New Jersey

New Jersey does not require manufacturers to be licensed or bonded. All THOW dealers need to be licensed and have a $10,000 bond.

Dealers Licensing: https://www.state.nj.us/mvcbiz/BusinessServices/Dealership.htm
Motor Vehicle Department: https://www.nj.gov/mvc/
Form a corporation: https://www.njportal.com/dor/businessformation/home/welcome
Business startup: https://business.nj.gov/category/start

New Mexico

New Mexico does not require manufacturers to be licensed or bonded. All THOW dealers need to be licensed and have a $50,000 bond.

Dealers Licensing: http://www.mvd.newmexico.gov/mvd-related-businesses.aspx
Motor Vehicle Department: https://dot.state.nm.us/
Form a corporation: https://www.sos.state.nm.us/business-services/start-a-business/domestic-nm-llc/

Business startup:
https://www.sos.state.nm.us/business-services/start-a-business/

New York

New York does not require manufacturers to be licensed or bonded. N.Y. VEH. & TRAF. LAW 415 requires manufacturer to register with the NY Motor Vehicle Commission. All THOW dealers need to be licensed and have a $10,000-$25,000 bond, depending on sales volume.

Manufacturers Licensing:
Dealers Licensing:
https://dmv.ny.gov/forms/cr78.pdf & https://dmv.ny.gov/original-facility-application
Motor Vehicle Department: https://dmv.ny.gov/
Form a corporation: https://www.dos.ny.gov/corps/
Business startup: https://esd.ny.gov/startup-ny-program

North Carolina

North Carolina requires all manufacturers to be licensed and bonded ($50,000 bond). All THOW dealers need to be licensed and have a $50,000 bond.

Manufacturers Licensing:
https://law.justia.com/codes/north-carolina/2015/chapter-20/article-12
Dealers Licensing:
https://connect.ncdot.gov/business/DMV/DMV%20Documents/VS-400%20New%20Dealer%20License%20or%20Changes%20to%20Existing%20License%20-%20June%202020.pdf
Motor Vehicle Department:

https://www.ncdot.gov/dmv/offices-services/online/Pages/default.aspx
Form a corporation:
https://edpnc.com/start-or-grow-a-business/start-a-business/business-forms/
Business startup:
https://www.nc.gov/services/starting-business-nc

North Dakota

North Dakota does not require manufacturers to be licensed or bonded. All THOW dealers need to be licensed and have a $10,000-$25,000 bond.

Dealers Licensing:
http://www.dot.nd.gov/forms/sfn02932.pdf
Motor Vehicle Department:
https://www.dot.nd.gov/public/
Form a corporation:
http://www.nd.gov/eforms/
Business startup:
http://www.nd.gov/businessreg/

Ohio

Ohio does not require manufacturers to be licensed or bonded. All THOW dealers need to be licensed but not bonded.

Dealers Licensing:
https://publicsafety.ohio.gov/static/bmv4322.pdf
Motor Vehicle Department:
https://www.bmv.ohio.gov/#gsc.tab=0
Form a corporation:
https://www.sos.state.oh.us/businesses/filing-forms--fee-schedule/
Business startup:
https://ohio.gov/wps/portal/gov/site/business/resources/business-first-stop

Oklahoma

Oklahoma requires all manufacturers to be licensed but not bonded. THOW dealers need to be licensed but not bonded.

Manufacturers Licensing: https://www.ok.gov/omvc/documents/mfgdist_initial%20packet.pdf

Dealers Licensing: https://www.ok.gov/omvc/Forms/

Motor Vehicle Commission: https://www.ok.gov/omvc/index.html

Form a corporation: https://www.sos.ok.gov/corp/filing.aspx

Business startup: https://www.okcommerce.gov/doing-business/startups-entrepreneurs/how-to-start-a-business/

Oregon

Oregon does not require manufacturers to be licensed or bonded. All THOW dealers need to be licensed and have a $40,000 bond.

Dealers Licensing: https://www.oregon.gov/ODOT/Forms/DMV/370grp.pdf & https://www.oregon.gov/ODOT/DMV/pages/dealers/dealerbecome.aspx

Motor Vehicle Department: https://www.oregon.gov/odot/DMV/Pages/index.aspx

Form a corporation: https://sos.oregon.gov/business/Pages/domestic-business-corporation-forms.aspx

Business startup: https://sos.oregon.gov/business/pages/starting-business.aspx

Pennsylvania
> Pennsylvania requires all manufacturers to be licensed and carry a $20,000 bond per each place of business. Likewise, all THOW dealers must be licensed and carry a $20,000 bond per place of business
>
> Manufacturers & Dealer Licensing: https://www.dos.pa.gov/ProfessionalLicensing/BoardsCommissions/VehicleManufacturersDealersandSalespersons/Pages/Aplication-Forms.aspx
>
> Motor Vehicle Department: https://www.dmv.pa.gov/Pages/default.aspx
>
> Form a corporation: https://www.dos.pa.gov/BusinessCharities/Business/Resources/Pages/Pennsylvania-Business-Corporations.aspx
>
> Business startup: https://www.revenue.pa.gov/FormsandPublications/FormsforBusinesses/BusinessRegistration/Documents/rev-588.pdf

Rhode Island
> Rhode Island requires all manufacturers to be licensed but not bonded. All THOW dealers need to be licensed and have a $50,000 bond.
>
> Manufacturers Licensing: http://www.dmv.ri.gov/documents/forms/business/New_RenewalApplicationForDistributorManufacturerOrRepresentative.pdf
>
> Dealers Licensing: http://www.dmv.ri.gov/documents/forms/business/FirstApplicationForDealership.pdf
>
> Motor Vehicle Department: http://www.dmv.ri.gov/

Form a corporation: https://www.sos.ri.gov/divisions/business-services
Business startup: https://www.ri.gov/SOS/quickstart/help/

South Carolina

South Carolina does not require manufacturers to be licensed or bonded. All THOW dealers need to be licensed and, THOW-RV dealers require a $15,000 bond, and THOW-MH dealers require a $30,000 bond.

Dealers Licensing: http://www.scdmvonline.com/Business-Customers/Dealers/Dealer-Licenses & http://www.scdmvonline.com/Business-Customers/Dealers/Dealer-Licenses/Surety-Bond

Motor Vehicle Department: http://scdmvonline.com/

Form a corporation: https://businessfilings.sc.gov/BusinessFiling/Home/DownloadForms?pdfCategoryId=1&category=Starting%20a%20Business%20in%20South%20Carolina

Business startup: https://scbos.sc.gov/starting

South Dakota

South Dakota does not require manufacturers to be licensed or bonded. All THOW dealers need to be licensed and have a $25,000 bond.

Manufacturers Licensing:

Dealers Licensing: http://www.scdmvonline.com/Business-Customers/Dealers/Dealer-Licenses

Motor Vehicle Department: https://dor.sd.gov/

Form a corporation: https://sdsos.gov/business-services/corporations/corporate-forms/default.aspx

Business startup: https://sd.gov/business.aspx

Tennessee

Tennessee requires all manufacturers to be licensed but not bonded. All THOW dealers need to be licensed and have a $50,000 bond.

Manufacturers Licensing: https://apps.tn.gov/licenses-app/view?id=908

Dealers Licensing: https://apps.tn.gov/licenses-app/view?id=1201

Motor Vehicle Department: https://www.secstates.com/TN_DMV_Tennessee_Department_of_Motor_Vehicles

Form a corporation: https://sos.tn.gov/business-services/business-entity-filings

Business startup: https://www.tn.gov/content/dam/tn/ecd/documents/bero/TNSmartStartupGuide.pdf

Texas

Texas requires all manufacturers to be licensed but not bonded. All dealers need to be licensed and have a $25,000 bond. To manufacture THOW-RV (in Texas known as travel trailer or motorhomes) you must get a Manufacturer license from Texas DMV:

https://www.txdmv.gov/dealer/manufacturer

Manufacturers cannot operate, control or own an interest in a dealership. See TEXAS OCCUPATIONS CODE §2301.476 for details and exceptions. Texas offers another type of license called a Converter license. However, these do not apply to motorhomes. And like a manufacturers license, a converter licensee is not allowed to operate a dealership or sell their products to the public.
https://www.txdmv.gov/dealer/converter
There is one exception, if you are not manufacturing the vehicle, instead you are making "after-market" modifications to a vehicle that was already sold through a retail outlet, then the conversions are not regulated by Texas DMV.
To sell THOWs you must first become licensed then start a dealership. The process of applying for a license starts here:
https://texasdmv.force.com/customers/lace_login
After obtaining a license, you can apply to open a dealership. Here's information on how to start a dealership:
https://www.txdmv.gov/dealers/licensing/what-you-need-to-know-about-starting-your-new-dealership
Regulations about advertising:
https://www.txdmv.gov/dealers/dealer-services/dealer-tips
Texas DMV's information for RV customers:

https://www.txdmv.gov/sites/default/files/body-files/SmartBuyer_SmartRV.pdf

If you plan to sell THOW-RVs in Texas, the Texas RV Association website has information about becoming a dealer, supplies, manufacturers, finance, insurance, and much more: https://trva.org/membership/benefits/

Utah

Utah requires all manufacturers to be licensed but not bonded. All dealers need to be licensed and have a $75,000 bond.

Manufacturers Licensing: https://mved.utah.gov/licenses/manufacturer

Dealers Licensing: https://mved.utah.gov/licenses/dealer

Motor Vehicle Department: https://mved.utah.gov/

Form a corporation: https://www.utah.gov/business/starting/structure_starting.html

Business startup: https://www.utah.gov/business/starting.html

Vermont

Vermont does not require manufacturers to be licensed or bonded. All THOW dealers need to be licensed and have a $20,000-$35,000 bond.

Dealers Licensing: https://dmv.vermont.gov/enforcement-and-safety/dealer-services

Motor Vehicle Department: https://dmv.vermont.gov/

Form a corporation: https://sos.vermont.gov/corporations/

Business startup: https://tax.vermont.gov/business-and-corp/start-a-business

Virginia

Virginia requires all manufacturers to be licensed but not bonded. All THOW dealers need to be licensed and have a $25,000 bond.

Manufacturers Licensing: https://www.dmv.virginia.gov/commercial/#dealer/mnfdist.asp

Dealers Licensing: https://mvdb.virginia.gov/h-t-b-dealer/

Motor Vehicle Department: https://www.dmv.virginia.gov/#/

Form a corporation: https://www.scc.virginia.gov/pages/Entity-Formation-and-Registration-Documents

Business startup: https://www.sbsd.virginia.gov/virginia-small-business-financing-authority/

Washington

Washington requires all manufacturers to be licensed have a $20,00 bond. All THOW dealers need to be licensed and have a $30,000 bond.

Manufacturers & Dealer Resource manual: https://www.dol.wa.gov/business/vehiclevesseldealer/docs/DealerManual.pdf

Business Licensing: https://dor.wa.gov/get-form-or-publication/forms-subject/business-licensing-forms

Startup business: https://dor.wa.gov/open-business/new-business-information

Motor Vehicle Department: https://wsdot.wa.gov/
Form a corporation: https://www.sos.wa.gov/corps/forms.aspx

West Virginia

West Virginia requires all manufacturers to be licensed but not bonded. All THOW dealers need to be licensed and have a $25,000 bond.

Manufacturers Licensing: see dealer licensing page

Dealers Licensing: https://transportation.wv.gov/DMV/Dealers/Pages/Dealers-Licensing.aspx & https://transportation.wv.gov/DMV/Dealers/Pages/default.aspx

Form a corporation: https://sos.wv.gov/business/pages/RegNewWVBus.aspx

Transportation: https://transportation.wv.gov/Pages/default.aspx

Wisconsin

Wisconsin requires all manufacturers to be licensed but not bonded. All THOW dealers need to be licensed and have a $50,000 bond.

Manufacturers Licensing: https://wisconsindot.gov/Pages/dmv/dlr-agents/busns-lcnse/manufacturerlicense.aspx

Dealers Licensing: https://wisconsindot.gov/Pages/dmv/dlr-agents/busns-lcnse/recreationdlr.aspx

Business startup & form a corporation: http://wilawlibrary.gov/topics/comlaw/

Transportation:
https://wisconsindot.gov/Pages/home.aspx

Wyoming

Wyoming requires all THOW manufacturers and all dealers to be licensed and carry a $25,000 bond. Wyoming does not have a corporate income tax or a personal income tax.

Dealers & Manufacturers Licensing:
http://www.dot.state.wy.us/files/live/sites/wydot/files/shared/Motor%20Vehicle%20Services/Final_Dealer_%26_Mfg_App_Requirements.pdf

Bonding:
http://www.dot.state.wy.us/files/live/sites/wydot/files/shared/Compliance_and_Investigation/WY-Based%20Manufacturer%20Bond%20Form.pdf

Business licensing:
https://www.wyomingbusiness.org/content/licensing-and-permitting

Form a corporation:
https://sos.wyo.gov/Business/Default.aspx

Transportation:
http://www.dot.state.wy.us/home.html

CHAPTER 3

CONTRACTS TO SELL TINY HOMES

As explained in the last chapter, Dealer- and Manufacturer-licensing requirements are different in every state. Likewise, contract law is specific to each state. However, there are some parts of a contract that are common to all. As a starting place, I am going to explain the common contract clauses, for manufacturers, to make sure your contract has, at least, the minimum requirements. However, once you have these you should go to a contract lawyer in your state to make sure your contract meets your state's requirements for a vehicle purchase agreement.

It is a statutory requirement that certain agreements must be in writing. Although these vary from state to state, anytime there is work greater than $500, it should be written. A written document will not be forgotten like a verbal agreement and is more likely to keep the parties aware of their rights and responsibilities. If there is a dispute and an arbitrator or judge is asked to interpret the agreement, they are more likely to find in accordance with your true intent if that intent is in writing.

One of the biggest sources of disputes is change orders and extras. To determine if something is in addition to or outside the scope of the original agreement, you must be able to accurately determine what the original agreement states. If the original agreement is well defined and in writing, it will be much easier to determine if something is added or changed. Once you determine that a request is different than what was agreed to (whether more or less), document that fact in writing. You should also immediately negotiate the effect of the change, such as cost and time. Tell your customer the new cost and allow the customer to determine if the change is worth it. If you and your customer agree to the change, make sure both parties sign the written change order.

Parts of a contract

1. Title - this goes at the top of the contract and briefly explains what the contract is for; something like "Tiny Home Purchase Agreement" or "Custom Tiny Home Purchase Agreement."
2. Names of all parties – this would be the name of your company, which should be a corporation to protect yourself from liability, and the name(s) and address(es) of buyer(s). Near you name should be your license number(s) and the agency that issued your license(s). For example, Joe's Tiny Homes Inc. CA DMV #MP9873641. And after each party's name there should be a description of their role in this transaction. From this point forward, the contract will use the role not the name.
3. Date the agreement is written. Sometimes the date it is written and the date it is signed are different. If they are different, there should be language explaining

which date is the "effective date," somewhere in the agreement.
4. The above two are combined into a sentence that is the purpose of the contract. For example: "This is an agreement between Joe's Tiny Homes Inc. CA DMV #MP9873641 (Dealer) and Julia Gonzalez, 123 State St., Berkeley CA (Buyer), for the purchase of a custom tiny home on wheels on June 15, 2022 (effective date)."

Legal requirements – Part of the agreement must explain the Buyer's rights and other government-required notices. These vary from state to state.

5. The right of recission – buyers have a right to change their mind after signing a contract for a vehicle. If they change their mind within the "buyer's remorse" time, it's as if they never signed the contact. You have to give them back any deposit they gave you. Never start building or purchasing materials until after the recission period has passed. The contract must tell them how long they have to change their mind, called the Right to Recission.
6. Change Orders – If the tiny homes you build are custom made, then it is very likely your buyers will be changing their mind about how it is built during the build process. Your contract must explain the change-order process. There should be a written request form they fill in and a Dealer-response form indicating whether the change increases, decreases or if the

price stays the same based on the requested change. The contract should explain the change-order process.
7. Motor Vehicle Department requirements – these are the requirements to issue a vehicle registration, the forms vary from state to state. Here are some example forms.
    a. If the THOW will be registered in a different state than it's built you will need a special form. In Florida it is called, Declaration Affidavit for MV Which Will be Titled in Another State/Country. In California, it is the Application for Title or Registration.
    b. Application for title or registration from DMV - this is the application form for vehicles being registered for the first time.
    c. Temporary license plate form
    d. Bill of Sale – this is a form from the DMV that identifies the vehicle by VIN, year and model. The seller and buyer are identified, and the seller transfers the vehicle to the buyer by signing the form. For RVs the form may include the weight and/or a certificate of origin.
8. Credit requirements and disclosures – if you are allowing your Buyers to apply for loans to buy their THOW, there is a stack of documents that you and/or the lender must provide
    a. Credit disclosure form
    b. Credit application
    c. Pre-Sale Credit Disclosure – The federal Truth-in-Lending Act – or

"TILA" for short – requires that borrowers receive written disclosures about important terms of credit before they are legally bound to pay the loan.
   d. Risk Based Pricing Notice – Risk-based pricing occurs when lenders offer different consumers different interest rates or other loan terms, based on the estimated risk that the consumers will fail to pay back their loans. The form is given to all customers who finance.
   e. Notice of Credit Denial (Adverse Action Notice) – Regulation B and the Equal Credit Opportunity Act require creditors to provide consumers with nine notifications of adverse action when credit is denied. Automotive dealers are considered creditors under this act.
9. Other state requirements – when you get your Dealer and Manufacturer licenses from your state, you will get a package of forms and booklets that explain the state's requirements. For example, Florida requires Florida Statutes Section 501.98, Notice which gives notice to customers that before bringing any claim against a dealer they must give a 30-day notice.
10. IRS Form 8300 – a report for cash payments over $10,000
11. Lemon Law Notice – described in more detail in the following chapter

12. Any other consumer protection notices that are required for vehicle sales in your state

Purchase Agreement Terms
13. The THOW description, model name, vin #
14. Description of the THOW as described on the website, in advertising or any other place it's advertised.
15. Special options and accessories and their prices. This should include all the parts that are special requests, and things like color, design techniques, etc. If a Buyer requests something, put it in writing so they cannot later claim they didn't know they were getting a purple sink or two-burner stove.
16. The whole price of the THOW
17. Course of performance - The milestones for work and the associated payments. For example, if there are five payments, there will be a description of what work will be completed, and the supplies purchased at the time of each payment. There should also be a way for the customer to accept or reject each step. Each milestone should have a tentative completion date.
18. The completion date for the whole project
19. Explanation for delays and how Buyer will be notified if there are any delays
20. Payment terms – how and when payments will be made. Whether you accept credit cards, Venmo, PayPal, bank transfers, checks, money orders, etc. Where they should be mailed or your

bank account routing and account numbers or Venmo ID.
21. Consequences of non-payment
22. Arbitration Agreement -this is critical to avoid being sued and dragged through court for many years by an unhappy Buyer. Every party, the Dealer and the Buyer must initial right below the arbitration clause.
23. Warranties – a description of the warranties' duration and terms, a list of systems and labor that are covered, must be completely explained. Things that are not covered by the warranty should also be explained. Express written warranties are covered in state law and may include explanation of when warranty periods can be lengthened. Repair or replacement options.
24. Right of buyer to inspect THOW

Other Legal Clauses
25. Merger or Integration clause – says that this written agreement is the entire agreement between the parties no matter what was said prior to this writing. And requires that all future agreements and changes must be in writing.
26. Notice – this will have the contact information for all parties, including the names, email and mailing address so that if there is a lawsuit this is where the parties will receive service.
27. Force majeure - says that if something drastic goes wrong a delay in performance is excused. This should be updated to include health pandemics including Covid outbreaks which have

crippled many businesses and supply chains.
28. Attorney Fees -if there is a legal battle who pays for each party's lawyer
29. Choice of law – this explains which state laws will apply and which venue will be used for disputes
30. Enforceability of contract – says that if any part of the contract is found to be unenforceable by the court, the rest of the contract remains in force
31. Electronic signatures agreement
32. Signatures – remember that your signature will have your name, your title and the name of the company since you are signing in your role as a representative of the company, each signature should have a date signed, and it's helpful to include contact information beneath each signature

Non-Custom Manufacturing

What if you are not building custom tiny homes? Instead, you are building all your tiny homes based on one or two models. In that situation, you would not need the parts of the Purchase Agreement Terms related to customization. Sections 15 would be eliminated if there were no options. Section 17 could be eliminated if the customer is not privy to the course of building and will buy a home that comes off the assembly line. Sections 18 & 19 might also be eliminated under those sorts of circumstances. The other parts of the sales agreement would still be required according to your state's laws.

In addition to providing a purchase contract to buyers, be prepared to deliver the warranties for components included like the oven, microwave, refrigerator, air conditioner, composting toilet, and trailer, etc.

CHAPTER 4

LEMON LAWS

Not all tiny homes are created equally. The problem is that some are not made well. Buyers of THOWs are probably protected by the RV-buyer-protection laws called lemon laws. Manufacturers should know about these laws to protect themselves from having to buy back the THOW after it's completed. Lemon laws are state laws that provide a remedy for buyers of vehicles, including cars and RVs that repeatedly fail to meet standards of quality and performance. The manufacturer or dealer must compensate the buyer for the faulty products.

When is an RV considered a lemon? In order to be considered a faulty or lemon RV:

- The THOW must still be under warranty but have faced two failed attempts at fixing an issue.
- The THOW must now be worth much less since the inconvenience persisted and it isn't functional.
- The THOW started showing issues within the first 18 months or 18,000 miles.

Which states have RV lemon laws?

This list explains what has to go wrong to allow the Buyer to take legal action to declare that the THOW is a lemon in each state. Here are the lists of each US state and what qualifies as a lemon in each. States can have restrictions on weight, days out of service and the number of attempts you've made at fixing the issue.

1. 3-4 unsuccessful repair attempts within the warranty period. - Alabama / Colorado / Connecticut / District of Columbia / Indiana / Iowa / Kentucky / Maryland / Massachusetts / Michigan / Nevada / North Dakota / Oregon / Pennsylvania / Rhode Island / South Dakota / Tennessee
2. 3-4 unsuccessful repair attempts and a certain number of days out of service. - Alaska / Illinois / Maine / Mississippi / Montana / New York / Nebraska / New Jersey / South Carolina / Vermont / Virginia / Washington / West Virginia
3. 3-4 unsuccessful repair attempts, a certain number of days out of service, and must be under a certain weight. - Arizona / Arkansas / California / Delaware / Louisiana / Missouri / Utah / Wisconsin / Georgia / Hawaii / New Hampshire / New Mexico / North Carolina / Oklahoma / Wyoming
4. 4 unsuccessful repair attempts, has spent 60 days out of service and covers non-living areas of RV only. - Florida
5. 3-4 unsuccessful repair attempts, a certain number of days out of service plus

may cause serious bodily harm. - Idaho / Minnesota* / Ohio**

6. Applies only to the chassis. - Arkansas / California / Delaware / Louisiana / Missouri / Utah / Wisconsin / Georgia / Hawaii / Idaho / Kansas / Minnesota / Mississippi / Montana / New York / New Jersey / South Carolina / Vermont / Virginia / Washington / West Virginia

*No certain number of days out of service
**Except facilities used for sleeping and eating

In California, the lemon law is actually named Song-Beverly warranty Act. It says that if the manufacturer or dealer is not able to meet the terms in an express written warranty after three or four repair attempts, the manufacturer is required to promptly replace the vehicle or return the full purchase price to the buyer. If the buyer has to hire an attorney, they are entitled to attorney's fees, which could be as much as the THOW. Bottom line – if there are problems with the product you built, fix it fast and in the fewest number of repair attempts as possible.

CHAPTER 5

THOW BUILDING STANDARDS

As I explained above, there are three classes of homes on wheels. Two of these are 400 square feet or smaller and are considered tiny homes. Tiny Homes on wheels, THOWs, are currently being built using RV-industry building standards and following the RV industry's definitions. The RV industry defined larger units for short-term living called Park Models; and small vehicles which move around and are used for weekend vacations called trailers, campers and fifth wheels.

The tiny home industry has blurred the lines which distinguish these classes by building small THOWs as permanent housing. To make it even more confusing, our industry has blurred the lines between housing on foundations which are regulated by local building codes and international building codes (IBC) with the vehicle standards used to build RVs. In legal terms, building tiny homes doesn't exactly conform to any of the laws, codes or standards. In non-legal terms, it's a big mess. Here are the RV standards which should be the minimum requirements used to build THOWs.

Classification	Structure	Regulating Agency	Regulations
Recreational vehicle (RV)	On chassis with wheels	3rd party inspector approved by State's housing department and registered with MV Dept	NFPA 1192 or ANSI Standard A119.5, IBC Appendix Q
Park model (PM)	On chassis with or without wheels	3rd party inspector approved by State's housing department and registered with MV Dept	ANSI A119.5 and NFPA 1192 including NFPA 70

Here are the distinctions of the RV types of THOWs based on design style

RV Industry Class	THOW classification	Description	Size
Travel trailer or camper (In Calif called Conventional RV)	THOW-RV	Most can be towed with a regular-sized vehicle. A larger model may require a heavier pickup or van as the towing vehicle.	vary in length from 13 to 35 feet
Fifth wheel	THOR-RV	Is coupled to the towing vehicle (usually a pickup truck) with a hitch centered over the vehicle's rear axle.	vary in length from 17 to 40 feet
Park Model	THOW-PM	Transported on a chassis on wheels, wheels may be removed during set up.	under 400 square feet in set-up mode

THOW-PMs and THOW-RVs have several structural, design, and occupancy differences. But relating to regulations and compliance, they're subject to many of the same standards.

To be occupiable, THOW-PMs must be constructed to ANSI A119.5 and NFPA 1192 standards and must be certified by the manufacturer with a label of approval from a 3rd-party certification company. NFPA 1192 includes the National Electrical Code 2020 NFPA 70 (NFPA 70).

ANSI A119.5, the Park Model RV standard requirements apply in the following states: Alabama, Arizona, California, Colorado, Connecticut, Delaware, Florida, Georgia, Idaho, Kentucky, Michigan, Missouri, Montana, Nebraska, Nevada, New Jersey (with some adjustments), North Dakota, Ohio, Oregon (with some adjustments), Pennsylvania, Rhode Island, South Dakota, Tennessee, Texas, and Washington. States without regulations as of 2014, include Alaska, Arkansas, Georgia, Hawaii, Illinois, Indiana, Iowa, Kansas, Louisiana, Maine, Maryland, Massachusetts, Minnesota, Mississippi, New Hampshire, New Mexico, New York, North Carolina, Oklahoma, South Carolina, Utah, Vermont, Virginia, West Virginia, Wisconsin and Wyoming. See https://dta0yqvfnusiq.cloudfront.net/2020s28168124/2018/06/Park-Model-RV-Standard-Req-by-State-5b355943f13e7.pdf for the 2014 state-by-state list of the laws and regulations.

When each state adopts the latest version of the regulations to become state law, they are renumbered to fit that state's coding system. In **California**, THOW-PM laws are defined in Ann. Cal. Health & Safety Code §18027.3(a)(2) §18009.3 §18033 §18033.1. In **Florida**, they are defined in F.S.A. § 320.8231 (1); F.S.A. § 320.822 (1)(b) and (18)(b). In **Michigan** they are defined in Mich. Admin. Code R. 325.1551(d); M.C.L.A. 257.38a. In **Oregon** they are defined in OAR 918-525- 0040; OAR 918-525- 0310. In **Texas** they are defined in V.T.C.A., Tax Code § 11.14 (b)(2); V.T.C.A., Property Code § 94.001(8); 43 TX ADC § 217.3

(a)(5)(C)(iv). You must check your state's regulations to verify which version of the standards apply.

ANSI Standard A119.5

The American National Standards Institute (ANSI) A119.5 Park Model RV Standard is published on a five-year cycle. The latest ANSI A119.5 Park Model RV Standard became effective September 1, 2020, with an enforcement date of January 1, 2021. Below, I provide links to buy the latest standards. In addition to selling these standards, the RVIA Standards Department produces a handbook for each of the standards. Manufacturers of THOW-PMs should consider buying both the standard and the handbook which includes more than 200 illustrations and an array of tables and charts explaining the building steps.

This set of rules regulates minimum building and safety requirements for construction, electrical, plumbing, fuel burning, and safety-related systems in a Park Model RV. They provide general do's and don'ts, such as "Park Model RVs shall not be equipped with gasoline or diesel fuel storage and fuel transfer or dispensing systems," and "Park Model RVs shall not be equipped with internal combustion engine generators or preparations for the later installation of an internal combustion engine generator."

They also have very specific rules such as:
- Requirements for curtains located within certain distance of flammable areas,

- Requirements for interior finish flame spread limitations,
- Fire extinguisher location requirements,
- Plumbing support intervals requirements,
- Ventilation requirements, and
- The weight limit for ladders to a loft.

    The 2020 edition of ANSI 119.5 regulations enforcement began on January 1, 2021. These have many changes from the previous edition. Here are some general descriptions of the additional rules which apply to THOW-PM:

- Murphy beds can be used with specific safety requirements for securing them in the up and down positions.
- Each THOW-PM may carry up to 4 DOT, removable, manufacturer-installed, 45-lb cylinders for propane.
- Owners' manuals can be on PDF, online, digital (CD or DVD), or printed.
- Potable water tanks filled from city water must have a vent with specific size piping and venting.
- Potable water tanks must have structural support capable of holding twice the filled weight in all directions except up.
- Instructions for potable water tanks must include the tank installation instructions.
- Waste holding tanks must have specified structural supports. And the installation instructions must explain securing requirements.
- Black water holding tank must have a continuous vent.
- Flush toilets are a big deal. Usually, flush toilets do not lead to a black-water tank.

However, when there is a holding tank, there are a lot of plumbing specifications to make sure the black water does not back up into the toilet, shower or tub.
- Backwater valves must be used in certain plumbing configurations to prevent blackwater from flowing up into showers/tubs from over-filled holding tanks.
- Roof vent pipe extensions are reduced in height above the roofline, from previous regulations. Vents cannot terminate in other ways like along walls. They must be above the roofline.
- Potable water systems must be tested in a two-step process using pressurized air or water. And a second step isolates different parts of the system tested at specific pressures.
- New rules about connected lofts, including requirements for guard rails, stairs, ventilation, light, exits, safety and fire detection equipment.
- Loft guard rails must be permanent, not removable. And the rules are specific about the size of ladders gaps in the guard rails for movable ladders.
- Decking materials (for decks and handrails) made of plastic composites must comply with specific requirements.

The complete 2020 set of ANSI Standard A119.5 rules is available from RVIA for $45, and the Handbook which details the standard is $250

https://my.rvia.org/store?category=a0L410000075wYaEAI&_ga=2.19738737.879179216.1609114246-763916367.1609114246
IHS Markit for $77.
https://global.ihs.com/doc_detail.cfm?document_name=ANSI%20A119%2E5&item_s_key=00146363

Do yourself a favor and buy the Handbook. This isn't the place to skimp.

NFPA 1192

NFPA stands for National Fire Protection Agency. The entire standard is a sixty-four-page copyrighted document and can be purchased for $58 from NFPA.
https://www.nfpa.org/codes-and-standards/all-codes-and-standards/list-of-codes-and-standards/detail?code=1192
Or purchased from the RVIA website for $58.
https://my.rvia.org/NC__Product?id=a1B41000003jdmGEAQ

It can be viewed for free from the NFPA website, https://www.nfpa.org/codes-and-standards/all-codes-and-standards/list-of-codes-and-standards/detail?code=1192.

A THOW-RV CHASSIS FOR A CONVENTIONAL CAMPER-STYLE RV. THIS CHASSIS ONLY HAS TWO WHEELS ON EACH SIDE WHICH LIMITS THE SIZE AND WEIGHT OF THE THOW IT CAN CARRY. SOME CHASSES HAVE 3 OR 4 WHEELS PER SIDE FOR LARGER THOWS. TRAILERS SHOULD HAVE A VIN NUMBER AND A CERTIFICATION DECAL. EACH TRAILER ALSO HAS A WARRANTY WHICH SHOULD BE TRANSFERRED TO THE THOW BUYER.

Some of the important parts of NFPA 1192 are:

Chapter 3: Definitions
Chapter 4: General Requirements
   4.4.1. All Electrical Systems shall comply with Article 551 Part I and III through VI of NFPA 70
   4.4.2. Low voltage electrical systems shall comply with ANSI/RVIA LV
Chapter 5: Fuel Systems and Equipment
Chapter 6: Fire and Life Safety Provisions
  6.2. Means of Escape
   6.2.1.1. Each RV shall have one primary means of escape and at least one secondary means of escape
   6.2.1.2. Each sleeping area shall have at least two different routes of escape to the outside of the RV
Sample Warning Labels
  6.3.1 Smoke Alarms
  6.4.1 Fire Extinguishers

6.6.1.1.1. Stairways shall be not less than 17 inches in clear width
6.6.1.1.2. The minimum width below the handrail shall be not less than 20 inches
6.6.1.2.1. Treads shall be a minimum of 7 inches, risers shall be a maximum of 12 inches
Chapter 7: Plumbing Systems (Important!)
7.3.5. Installation of Piping
7.3.6. Water Supply Requirements
7.4. Drainage Systems
7.4.3. Connections
7.5. Waste Holding Tanks
7.6.4. Flush Toilet Venting
Chapter 8: Vehicular Requirements
8.6. Axle, Tire and Wheel Assembly Requirements for Towable Recreational Vehicles
Appendix A: Explanatory Material
Appendix B: Propane Pipe Sizing
Appendix C: Product Listing Standards
Appendix D: Informational References

Building Bigger?

Structures that may resemble THOW-PMs but exceed 400 square feet are considered either a manufactured home (MH), if their design and construction are consistent with HUD's manufactured housing standards, or they're classified as a nonconforming structure (for which occupancy is illegal) unless they meet other permitted standards approved by your state's housing department. If you're building bigger than allowed in the standards cited above, you will subject yourself too HUD law for mobile homes, which is a very complicated process requiring lots of compliance, fees, checks and certifications. That isn't covered in this handbook.

Building Codes

Because THOWs are built with the materials used in stick-built homes, some manufacturers are building according to International Building Codes (IBC) instead of or in addition to RV standards described above. The basic problem with that choice is that those techniques haven't yet been safety tested for the types of stress that vehicles must endure like traveling at 60 mph over a bumpy road for hours. Is it legal to build tiny homes on wheels using building codes? That depends on where you're located. If the jurisdiction where you manufacture the vehicles has an ordinance that allows building THOWs to building codes, then it is legal. If the jurisdiction has codes that specifically says that THOWs must be built to RV standards, then building to IBC violates the ordinance and is not legal. Sometimes it's not the state of jurisdiction building code that is most important. If the state of local code says that tiny homes must be built to one code, say ASNI 119.5, in order to be sold or lived in, then that is the code to follow. If there is no local ordinance, then a builder should follow the guidelines of the certification company from which it will be certified. If a manufacturer is building following IBC building codes, to protect yourself, you should have a contractor's license, to prove that you are proficient at those techniques. If you do not have a contractors license and you build to IBC, in California, you are committing a misdemeanor or felony depending on the price of the building project, and can be sued by the state's contractors license board.

CHAPTER 6

LEGAL DISPUTES

Sometimes you may have legal disputes. If the customer does not pay you money when it is due, you have the right to enforce your written agreement. You can greatly minimize the likelihood of a dispute by documenting your agreements, meeting problems head-on, seeking solutions, negotiating and documenting changes as they occur, communicating with your customer, and invoicing regularly. If you can't resolve a problem with reasonable effort to settle or an insurance claim, you may use small claims court, arbitration, or civil litigation a.k.a. a lawsuit.

Small Claims

If the amount they owe is small, it will be a small claims court matter. In California, the small claims court can award a monetary judgement up to $10,000. This limit varies from state to state. Small claims courts are fast and economical. Your claim can usually be heard within a few months and the court fees and cost should be minimal. Each party in a small claims matter represents themselves, so there are not lawyer fees. Small claims courts have an appeal process. If you are not happy with the judgment, you can appeal.

Arbitration

If your agreement has an arbitration clause this is another technique for settling disputes. in comparison to court proceedings, arbitration is fast and low cost. Arbitration is different from court proceedings in a number of ways. Both parties must agree to arbitration and can choose the arbitrator. Both parties will want to choose an arbitrator who is familiar with RV, vehicle or construction law. Either side may present its own case or use an attorney. Because its more informal, some of the rules in court, such as the rules of evidence, are not always followed. Arbitrators may allow much more evidence than would be allowed in court. Most arbitration decisions are binding (the arbitrator's decision is final). Finally, there are very few grounds for appeal of an arbitration decision. Once it's done and the decision is written, that is it. Arbitration decisions can be certified by the court to help with collections or delivered to a collections company.

Lawsuits

Like any other business, you can file suit for breach of a contract if someone does not fulfill their obligation. If a customer does not pay you money when it is due, you can sue them in court, unless you have an arbitration clause in the contract. It is a good idea to have an attorney represent you in court due to the technical requirements of the court procedures. Even simple lawsuits can stretch out for years and cost hundreds of thousands of dollars in legal fees.

I didn't mention insurance. Insurance is important and required for licensing in most states. It will be your safety net if something goes wrong. It's a lot easier to make an insurance claim than to fight a lawsuit, if you make an error or something else goes wrong.

CHAPTER 7

FAQs

Frequently Asked Questions

Q: I searched the motor vehicle department records to see which tiny home manufacturers have the required licenses and found that some are not licensed as required. Does that mean I do not need a license?

A: As of this date, January 2023, we are educating the builders and spreading the information about the license requirements and how to get licensed. Prior to this, most manufacturers started as small companies that did not know about license requirements. THOWs have existed in a gray area between traditional homes and RVs. Many builders have contractors' licenses that they previously believed was the required license to build tiny homes. Others have no license from their state and should not be building anything. Many are in the process of getting the vehicle manufacturers or dealers licenses.

    The state authorities that manage the vehicle-manufacturer-licensing process have not yet enforced the license requirements on tiny home manufacturers. However, with so many new manufacturers coming online, and most of the new ones eager to follow the laws, the momentum will move toward law enforcement. Certification companies are requiring their manufacturers to be licensed in order to obtain certifications for their THOWs. And, there have already been a number of lawsuits against unlicensed manufacturers who built dangerous tiny homes. The fact that they were unlicensed, in violation of state law, contributed to their losing in court.

Q: What is Regulation Z?

A: Regulation Z is a nationwide, consumer-protection law related to loans and lending. Sometimes it's called the "Truth In Lending Act" or TILA. It standardizes how lenders use lending documents which describe the cost of borrowing to consumers. The regulations help borrowers understand the details of a loan before they take the loan, and restrict lenders from doing things that are misleading. If your company is involved in financing your THOWs, you are required to comply with Regulation Z and provide a stack of documents which I described in the Contracts chapter, section 8. If you are recommending lenders, you should make sure they are complying with these regulations.

Q: Can I sell the used THOW that my neighbor used to live in?

A: Dealers who sell used vehicles may have to comply with different licensing requirements or additional requirements than dealers who sell new vehicles. Check the motor vehicle department licensing requirements in your state. In California, there is a different license for used car dealers. However, new car dealers are allowed to sell both new and used vehicles.

Q: I asked a friend of mine, who is a realtor to sell my tiny homes, because everyone knows realtors are great salespeople. Is this allowed?

A: Realtors are licensed by each state under a type of license that permits them to sell real property. Real property includes buildings that are permanently attached to ground by foundations, and mobile homes which are regulated by HUD. When a tiny home is already located on a property being sold, the realtor can sell it as part of the property. However, when the tiny home is not sold as part of a property, it is a vehicle. To sell vehicles requires a different type of salesperson license, not a real-estate salesperson license. That vehicle salesperson license is obtained from the motor vehicle department. The realtor, or anyone working as a THOW salesperson, should get the additional vehicle-salesperson license before selling any tiny home not affixed to property or collecting any compensation for selling a vehicle.

Q: People keep calling THOWs ADUs. What does ADU mean?

A: ADU is the acronym for Accessory Dwelling Unit. "Accessory" means a building in addition to, usually behind or beside, another building. "Dwelling" means the building is safe for sleeping in, and has areas for eating and a bathroom. Thus, an ADU is usually the second home on a single-family zoned lot, or another additional home on a multi-family zoned lot. In general, ADUs are usually buildings built on foundations, called granny units. We are working towards getting THOWs to be legalized as ADUs.

CHAPTER 8

CONCLUSION

"Every strike brings me closer to the next home run." — Babe Ruth

The information provided above is intended to be your legal guideposts. It is generalities and outlines. It requires the customized details which will be specific for your business, created by you and the professionals you hire to help you. Use the information in this book to point you in the right direction for each step, to run your business successfully. Those who take the necessary steps will have the tools and the team for success.

As I mentioned in the introduction, to succeed in manufacturing tiny homes, you have to price your products to cover all labor, materials, and overhead expenses, pay yourself a decent salary, and make a profit that will keep your company alive. Legal expenses like licensing fees, bonding, insurance, corporate filings, taxes, business permits, accounting and lawyer fees are normal overhead of all businesses operating legally. If some businesses operate legally while others sneak around the laws, the competition is not fair. The balancing factor is that the cost of getting caught breaking the laws is about 100 times higher than the cost of doing business legally. Fines, penalties, interest payments and possibly even jail time are the penalties for breaking these laws. If you get sued your legal fees will be shocking. So, if you're not incentivized by wanting to follow the law, perhaps you may respond more to fear of getting caught. The businesses which are following the laws are incentivized to report the bad players who are not playing fairly by paying their overhead. This weeding out of the bad guys will be the normal growing pains of a burgeoning industry. Success is peace of mind knowing that you don't have to worry because you've made the effort to do things right.

I hope this information is received as intended, to help you create the best businesses, the ones that rise to the top. Go build beautiful, safe tiny homes! Protect your personal assets, your customers and your business! Build your business legally!

NOTES

NOTES

www.ingramcontent.com/pod-product-compliance
Lightning Source LLC
Chambersburg PA
CBHW070303220526
45465CB00004B/1721